THE NEW

VEGETARIAN COOKBOOK

ELIZABETH CORNISH

THE NEW
VEGETARIAN COOKBOOK
ELIZABETH CORNISH

CHARTWELL
BOOKS, INC.

A QUINTET BOOK

Published by Chartwell Books Inc.,
A Division of Book Sales Inc.,
110 Enterprise Avenue,
Secaucus, New Jersey 07094

ISBN 0-89009-856-5

This book was designed and produced by
Quintet Publishing Limited
6 Blundell Street, London N7

Art Director Peter Bridgewater
Editor Nicholas Law
Photographer John Heseltine

Typeset in Great Britain by
Q.V. Typesetting Limited, London
Colour origination in Hong Kong by
Hong Kong Graphic Arts Company Limited, Hong Kong
Printed in Hong Kong by Leefung-Asco
Printers Limited

CONTENTS

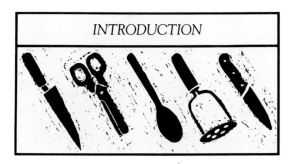

INTRODUCTION

Vegetarian food is different, delicious, nourishing and fresh. It can turn cooking, as well as eating, into a daily pleasure. The simple goodness of fresh ingredients in a loaf of home-made bread and a bowl of soup often give more satisfaction than the most complicated concoction smothered in butter-rich sauce. Learning to cook without meat and even fish is something of a challenge, so used are we all to having one or the other as the main dish of the meal.

Vegetarianism is enjoying a new surge of popularity in the developed world as a reaction to the high-fat, high-sugar, high-starch junk foods that have so dominated our diets for the past 30 years.

Many people choose to become vegetarian for reasons of health. A vegetarian diet is high in roughage and low in saturated fats. A lack of roughage in the Western diet has resulted in widespread intestinal problems. Saturated fats present in high levels in meat and dairy produce have been linked with heart disease.

Vegetarianism also makes economic and ecological sense. A field of soya beans will yield 30 times as much protein as the same field given over to the rearing of beef cattle. Surprisingly though, it is still the case that agricultural land is devoted to feeding animals, far more than to growing crops. A further cruel reality is that economic pressures tend to encourage under-developed countries to export their grain as cattle feed for richer countries.

Eggs, meat, potatoes, cream and butter (left) all contain a high level of saturated fat. All saturated fat contains cholesterol. The presence of too much cholesterol in the bloodstream can lead to a dangerous heart condition and possibly a heart attack.

For many people, the slaughter of animals for food is unacceptable, as is the practice of keeping battery hens in tiny cages for the duration of their short lives. Modern food production methods have effectively made meat much cheaper than ever before, but inevitably the taste of mass-produced meat, from animals reared on chemically treated feed and injected with hormones, suffers from a uniform blandness. A true free range chicken is practically impossible to buy in the Western world – in America 98 per cent of chickens are battery reared. As many vegetarians feel differently about fish, there is a section on fish in this book. Food processing robs us not only of one of the greatest pleasures of life – a wholesome natural taste – but it also takes with it roughage and many vitamins, replacing them with chemical additives, flavouring and colouring.

You don't have to be vegetarian to enjoy this book, but you might adopt a new attitude to eating. For instance, you could break away from the traditional three-course meal and serve several complementary dishes at once, as in Eastern countries, or you could serve one large salad as a main course and offer home-made bread and an assortment of dressings. The best thing about vegetarianism is that it is an adventure and opens new possibilities to the diner, and to the cook.

Brown rice, raw fruit, vegetables and breads are all excellent sources of fibre. A diet high in fibre will improve the efficiency of your digestive system.

Most fruits, particularly citrus fruits, are rich in vitamin C and the sugars in fruits are an instant and natural source of energy.

Carrots are particularly rich in vitamin A, which is also to be found in green leafy vegetables such as cabbage, along with vitamins B, C, E, and K and various minerals.

Wholemeal grains provide essential roughage for the digestive system and are a valuable source of vitamins B, E and K, as well as minerals.

Most vegetable oils are polyunsaturated fats, unlike animal fats which increase cholesterol — linked to heart disease — in the body.

Pulses such as lentils, dried peas, soya beans, chick peas and haricot beans provide vegetable protein and are also a source of vitamin B, iron and other minerals.

Fish is a particularly important source of protein and contains a wide range of essential vitamins and minerals.

Honey is a natural source of sugar and is rich in minerals such as calcium and magnesium.

Eggs, although high in cholesterol, are very rich in protein and contain vitamins and minerals in good quantities.

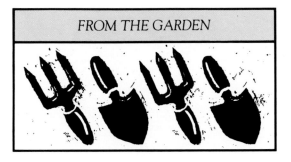

FROM THE GARDEN

CRUDITES WITH HOT ANCHOVY DIP

The crudités	
a selection of crisp raw vegetables, cut into manageable pieces	
carrots	
celery	
green, red and yellow peppers	
cucumber	
cauliflower florets	
radishes	
mushrooms	
The dip	
8 tbsp/100 g/4 oz butter	
2 cloves garlic, crushed	
8 anchovy fillets	
300 ml/10 fl oz thick (heavy) cream	

1 Prepare the vegetables and arrange them on a serving platter. Keep cold.

2 Prepare the dip. Heat the butter in a pan and add the garlic. Drain the anchovy fillets and pat dry with kitchen paper. When the garlic has softened, pound the anchovies into the pan until you have a smooth paste.

3 Beat in the cream and bring back to the boil. Cook, stirring, until the dip has thickened. Serve hot. If you use a small copper pan or a fondue pan, you can serve the dip in the pan you cooked it in.

175 g/6 oz pastry (enough for a single-crust pie) (see below)

1 tbsp butter

1 tbsp oil

550 g/1 lb 2 oz onions, finely chopped

2 eggs plus 1 yolk

450 ml/¾ pint single (light) cream

1-2 heaped tbsp grated Cheddar cheese

1-2 heaped tbsp chopped parsley

salt and freshly ground black pepper

pinch of cayenne pepper

1 Heat the oven to 190°C/375°F/Gas 5.

2 Line a 22-cm (8-in) quiche pan with the pastry.

3 Heat the butter and olive oil in a pan. Stir in the onions. Cover the pan, turn down the heat and sweat for about 5 minutes, stirring occasionally until soft and transparent.

4 Beat the eggs, cream and cheese together and add the onions and parsley. Season with salt, pepper and cayenne to taste, pour into the pastry crust and bake in the middle of the oven for 30-40 minutes until golden and set.

Onion and blue cheese tart

Combine 1-2 tbsp crumbled blue cheese with the cream before beating it with the eggs. Omit the Cheddar, parsley and cayenne pepper.

¾ cup/75 g/3 oz wholewheat flour

¾ cup/75 g/3 oz wholewheat (or white) self-raising (self-rising) flour

pinch of salt

6 tbsp/75 g/3 oz polyunsaturated margarine

water

1 Mix the flours and salt together in a bowl.

2 Cut the fat into small pieces in the flour and rub in with your fingertips until the mixture is fine and crumbly. Add enough water to bind together and roll into a smooth ball. Chill in the fridge for 20 minutes.

3 To use, roll the pastry out on a floured surface.

SPINACH AND CARROT TERRINE

1 Squeeze the spinach into a heavy-bottomed pan, cover and cook with only the water adhering to the leaves over a low heat for 5-8 minutes, stirring occasionally. When soft, allow to cool. Squeeze out the excess liquid and then purée in a blender.

2 Gradually beat the egg whites into the spinach. Add the salt, pepper, nutmeg and ginger. Stand the bowl over ice and beat in the cream a little at a time.

3 Cut up the carrots and cook in salted water until tender. Make up the carrot filling just as you made up the spinach filling.

4 Grease the terrine dish and carefully fill it with alternate layers of spinach and carrot mixture. Cover the dish with foil and stand it in a roasting tray of simmering water in the oven. Cook for 45 minutes. Allow to cool.

5 When the terrine is cool, cover the top of it with a layer of chaudfroid sauce. When this has set, decorate with a layer of carrot cutouts in an attractive pattern and glaze with aspic.

Aspic, carrageen and agar-agar

Commercial gelatine and aspic powders are made from the bones of animals and fish. Vegetarians who prefer not to use them can set foods with carageen or Irish moss, an edible seaweed available in powder form from health food shops. Another vegetable substitute for gelatine is agar-agar. Like gelatine, carageen and agar-agar come in varying strengths and you should follow the instructions on the pack when making them up. Neither imparts a taste to the finished dish.

Chaudfroid sauce

The spinach filling
1 kg/2 lb spinach, washed, stalks removed
2 egg whites
1 tsp salt
freshly ground white pepper
nutmeg
ground ginger
100 ml/4 fl oz double (heavy) cream

The carrot filling
400 g/14 oz carrots, peeled and trimmed
2 egg whites
1 tsp salt
freshly ground white pepper
100 ml/4 fl oz double (heavy) cream
butter to grease the terrine dish
250 ml/8 fl oz chaudfroid sauce (see below)
carrot cutouts to decorate
aspic to finish (see below)

Chaudfroid sauce
1 part thick mayonnaise to
2 parts cold but still liquid aspic or vegetable substitute (see above)
freshly ground white pepper

Combine the mayonnaise and aspic and mix well. Season with white pepper. (Black pepper will spoil the appearance of the sauce.)

Use the sauce to coat terrines, eggs and fish.

SUMMER POSY MOUSSE

The mousse

12 g/½ oz (2 envelopes) powdered gelatine
2 tbsp warm water
2 eggs, separated, plus 1 egg white
150 ml/5 fl oz double (heavy) cream
1 cup/100 g/4 oz Roquefort cheese, crumbled
3 tbsp soured (sour) cream
salt and freshly ground white pepper
a few drops of Tabasco sauce

The posy

nasturtium flowers and leaves
borage flowers and leaves
summer savoury
sprigs of mint, fennel and dill

1 Put the gelatine and water into a small bowl and stand it in a pan of simmering water. Stir well until the gelatine has dissolved.

2 Beat the egg yolks with half the double cream, the soured cream and the gelatine. Mash in the cheese. Whip the remaining double cream, fold into the mixture, season and add Tabasco sauce. Chill.

3 Whip the egg whites until soft peaks form. Fold them into the mixture. Oil a ring mould, pour in the mousse and chill until set.

4 Dip the mould into hot water, invert a plate over it and turn the mousse out. Fill the centre with a posy of edible flowers and delicate leafy herbs. This dish can form the centrepiece of a summer lunch in the garden. Serve with brown bread.

| 175 g/6 oz shortcrust pastry (enough for a single-crust pie) |
| 1 kg/2 lb spinach |
| 1 tbsp butter |
| salt and freshly ground black pepper |
| nutmeg |
| 300 ml/10 fl oz single (light) cream |
| 2 eggs plus 1 yolk |
| ½ cup/50 g/2 oz grated Parmesan cheese |
| 25-50 g/1-2 oz mushrooms, sliced |
| 1 tsp butter |

1 Preheat the oven to 190°C/375°F/Gas 5.

2 Wash the spinach and discard the tough stalks. Squeeze it into a large saucepan with the water still clinging to it and add the butter. Cook, tightly covered, over a low heat, stirring occasionally, until soft (about 5-8 minutes).

3 Purée the spinach in a blender and season to taste with salt, pepper and nutmeg.

4 Beat the cream, eggs and cheese together and stir in the spinach. Pour spinach mixture into a prepared pie crust and arrange the mushroom slices on top. Dot them with butter. Bake for 30-40 minutes until set and slightly browned on top.

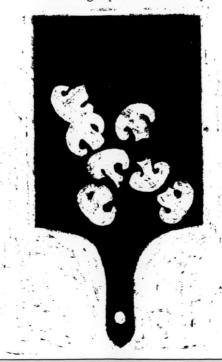

VEGETABLES IN ASPIC

600 ml/10 fl oz aspic or equivalent (see p 18)
1 cup peeled and diced carrot
1 cup trimmed and sliced green beans
1 tbsp walnut oil
1 cup sliced button mushrooms
1 tbsp stuffed olives, sliced
150 ml/5 fl oz thick mayonnaise

1 Prepare the aspic or equivalent (see p 18) and allow it to cool. Chill a mould. Wet the mould and when the aspic is almost set, line the mould with it. Place in the fridge to set.

2 Meanwhile cook the carrot and green beans in salted water until tender. Refresh in cold water. Heat the walnut oil in a pan and gently sauté the mushrooms. Allow to cool.

3 Mix the vegetables together with the olives, mayonnaise and the remaining aspic and fill the mould. Chill until set.

4 Dip the mould into hot water and turn out onto a plate. Cut into wedges and serve each wedge with a crisp lettuce leaf and a triangle of wholemeal (wholewheat) toast.

BROCCOLI AND TOMATO CHEESECAKE

The crumb base
1 cup/100 g/4 oz wholewheat biscuit (cracker) crumbs
4 tbsp/50 g/2 oz butter, softened
The filling
250 g/8 oz broccoli florets
1 large tomato
1½ cups/340 g/12 oz curd (cottage) cheese
salt and freshly ground white pepper
a pinch of nutmeg
2 eggs, separated
The topping
broccoli florets
a little gelatine if liked

1 Preheat the oven to 180°C/350°F/Gas 4.

2 Combine the crumbs and the butter and press down well into a greased 22-cm (8-in) quiche pan with a loose bottom.

3 Steam the broccoli florets over boiling salted water until tender. Carefully slice some of the florets for decorating and reserve the rest. Immerse the tomato in boiling water for a minute, refresh in cold water, peel and deseed.

4 Mash the curd cheese with the broccoli and tomato and season well with salt, pepper and a good pinch of nutmeg. Beat in the egg yolks.

5 Whisk the whites until they form soft peaks and fold into the mixture. Pour the filling over the crumb base and bake for about 20-25 minutes until slightly risen and just set.

6 Allow to cool. When cold, remove the sides of the tin and decorate the top with the remaining broccoli florets. Brush with gelatine if you like and chill before serving.

RUSSIAN POTATOES

1 kg/2 lb potatoes
salt and freshly ground black pepper
4 tbsp/50 g/2 oz butter
1 large onion, sliced
100 g/4 oz mushrooms, sliced
200 ml/6 fl oz soured (sour) cream
3 tbsp chopped chives

1 Scrub the potatoes and cook in salted water until barely tender. Drain, peel and slice.

2 Heat some of the butter in a flameproof casserole and fry the onion until translucent. Add the mushrooms and cook gently until the juices run. Add the rest of the butter as necessary and stir in the potatoes. Let them gently brown on one side, season, turn over and add the cream.

3 When most of the cream has been absorbed, sprinkle over the chopped chives and a little more pepper and serve.

STUFFED AUBERGINES (EGGPLANTS)

Serves 4 to 8

4 aubergines (eggplants)
olive oil
1 large onion, chopped
2-3 cloves garlic, crushed
4 large tomatoes, skinned and chopped
2 tbsp fresh herbs, chopped
salt and freshly ground black pepper
100 g/4 oz Mozzarella cheese
4 tbsp brown breadcrumbs
a little butter

1 Preheat the oven to 200°C/400°F/Gas 6.

2 Wash the aubergines. Cut in half lengthwise and score the cut surface deeply with a knife. Sprinkle with salt and leave, cut surface down, for 30 minutes.

3 Meanwhile, heat 1-2 tbsp oil in a pan and fry the onion and garlic until translucent. Transfer to a bowl and mix in the tomatoes and chopped herbs.

4 Add more oil to the pan. Rinse the aubergines and pat dry. Place them cut surface down in the pan and cook gently for about 15 minutes. They absorb a lot of oil, so you will need to keep adding a little more.

5 Scoop some of the flesh out of the aubergines, mash and mix it with the rest of the filling. Season well.

6 Pile the filling onto the aubergines and top with thinly sliced Mozzarella. Sprinkle with breadcrumbs and dot with butter. Place aubergines in a greased ovenproof dish and bake for 20 minutes until the cheese has melted and the breadcrumbs are crispy.

CREAM OF CAULIFLOWER SOUP

1 small cauliflower
salt and freshly ground black pepper
4 tbsp/50 g/2 oz butter
¼ cup/25 g/1 oz plain untreated (all-purpose) flour
120 ml/4 fl oz single (light) cream
1-2 egg yolks
1 tbsp chopped chives

1 Trim the outer leaves off the cauliflower and steam it whole in boiling salted water in a pan with the lid on until tender. Allow the cauliflower to cool and reserve the water.

2 Melt the butter in a saucepan and stir in the flour. Gradually stir in the cauliflower water, made up to 900 ml/30 fl oz with fresh water.

3 Reserve some of the cauliflower florets for garnishing. Discard the tougher stalks and purée the rest in a blender. Add to the saucepan.

4 Beat the cream and egg yolks together in a bowl. Beat in some of the soup, then return to the pan. Add reserved cauliflower florets. Heat through but do not boil. Season and add chopped chives. Serve with triangles of hot toast.

SALAD OF BROAD (LIMA) BEANS

A magnificent and very simple summer salad made with fresh young beans and peas. This combination of vegetables also tastes very good hot, if the beans and peas are not the first of the season.

340 g/12 oz unshelled broad (lima) beans
340 g/12 oz unshelled peas
4 small fresh Jerusalem artichokes
1-2 tbsp walnut oil or olive oil
1-2 tbsp lemon juice
garden mint
salt and freshly ground black pepper

1 Shell the beans and pod the peas. If they are not quite tender enough to eat raw, put them in a pan of boiling salted water for a minute, then refresh in cold water. Clean the artichokes, cut each into 6 and cook in boiling salted water for 5 minutes. Drain and refresh.

2 Make the dressing by blending the oil and lemon juice and adding chopped mint and seasoning to taste.

3 Toss the vegetables in the dressing and garnish with a few sprigs of mint. Serve with good crusty bread (try the Walnut bread on p 67).

WALDORF SALAD

Serves 2 to 4

8 stalks crisp celery

2 rosy-skinned dessert apples

lemon juice

½ cup/50 g/2 oz walnuts

6 tbsp good mayonnaise

salt and freshly ground black pepper

1 If the celery is not crisp, immerse it in ice-cold water. It will soon freshen up. Pat dry and slice.

2 Core the apples but do not peel – the pink skin will give colour contrast to the salad. Slice and sprinkle with lemon juice to prevent discolouring.

3 Toss all the ingredients in the mayonnaise and season well.

This salad also tastes good with blue cheese dressing. Blend the mayonnaise with 1 tbsp blue cheese before adding to the salad.

CAESAR SALAD

Serves 4 as a first course

The dressing

2 tbsp olive oil

2 tbsp white wine vinegar

1 clove garlic, crushed

salt and freshly ground black pepper

The salad

half a crisp Iceberg lettuce

4 eggs

4 anchovy fillets

1 cup/100 g/4 oz Roquefort cheese, crumbled

The croûtons

2 slices brown bread, crusts removed

2 tbsp olive oil

1 clove garlic, crushed

1 Make the dressing by combining the olive oil, vinegar, garlic and seasoning.

2 Break up the lettuce and divide between four salad plates. Soft boil the eggs and shell them under cold running water. Roll up the anchovy fillets. Put an egg and an anchovy fillet on each plate. Sprinkle the cheese over the top and pour the dressing over all.

3 To make the croûtons, cut the bread into small squares. Heat the oil in a pan, add the garlic and, when cooked, add the bread squares. Fry till golden. Divide between the plates. Cut into each egg so that the yolk can run out and serve straight away.

Caesar salad

FENNEL MORNAY

3 bulbs of fennel

bayleaf

The sauce

2 tbsp/25 g/1 oz butter

¼ cup/25 g/1 oz plain untreated (all-purpose) flour

300 ml/10 fl oz milk

150 ml/5 fl oz single (light) cream

1 cup/100 g/4 oz Cheddar cheese, grated

¼-½ cup/25-50 g/1-2 oz breadcrumbs

salt and freshly ground black pepper

1 Trim the fennel and simmer in salted water with a bayleaf for about 30 minutes until tender.

2 Meanwhile, make the sauce. Melt the butter in a pan and stir in the flour. Cook, stirring, for a couple of minutes and then gradually stir in the milk. Add the cream and most of the cheese and cook gently until the cheese has melted. Season well and keep warm.

3 Drain the fennel and cut each bulb in half. Lay the halves in a flameproof dish and pour the sauce over them. Sprinkle with the remaining cheese and the breadcrumbs. Put under a hot grill (broiler) to brown and melt the cheese.

For a tangier sauce, add a little powdered English mustard to taste.

PUMPKIN PIE

The pastry

1½ cups/175 g/6 oz wholewheat (or white) self-raising (self-rising) flour

pinch of salt

2 tbsp oil

water to mix

The filling

500 g/1 lb pumpkin flesh

4 eggs

150 ml/5 fl oz thick (heavy) cream

150 ml/5 fl oz milk

2 large tomatoes, peeled and chopped

1 tbsp chopped fresh basil leaves

freshly ground black pepper

1 Make the pastry. Sift the flour with the salt. Rub in the oil with your fingertips and add enough water to make a dough. Chill. Roll out. Line a greased 22-cm (8-in) quiche pan.

2 Preheat the oven to 190°C/375°F/Gas 5.

3 Remove rind and seeds from pumpkin and cut into slivers. Pack into a pan with very little water and cook over a low heat, covered. Check the pan occasionally to make sure the pumpkin hasn't dried out. After about 20 minutes you should be able to mash it into a purée.

4 Beat the eggs with the cream and milk. Mix in the pumpkin, tomato and basil and pour into the crust. Bake for 45 minutes until set and golden.

MUSHROOM-STUFFED ARTICHOKES

4 Jerusalem artichokes

juice of 1 lemon

2 tbsp/25 g/1 oz butter

1 clove garlic, crushed

250 g/8 oz mushrooms, chopped

1 tbsp pine kernels

2 tbsp chopped parsley

salt and freshly ground black pepper

1 Remove the artichokes' tough outer leaves and snip 2 cm (1 in) off the rest. Dip the cut edges of the leaves in lemon juice. Trim off the stalks and stand the artichokes upright in a large pan of boiling salted water. Simmer for 15 minutes. Drain upside down and allow to cool.

2 Meanwhile, make the filling. Heat the butter in a pan and cook the garlic until soft. Add the mushrooms. Cook gently until very black and juicy. Mix in the pine kernels and parsley and season with salt and pepper and a dash of lemon juice.

3 When the artichokes are cool, pull out the tiny leaves from the middle and the hairy inedible 'chokes' beneath them.

4 Spoon in the filling, closing the leaves over it. Put the artichokes in a greased ovenproof dish and heat through before serving.

SWISS POTATO CAKES

These crispy fried potato cakes can be served as an accompaniment or as a meal in themselves when topped with puréed spinach and a poached egg, or with a purée of root vegetables (see p 39) sprinkled with cheese and browned under the grill (broiler). You can vary the mixture by adding some grated onion or some grated cheese, or a bit of both.

500 g/1 lb waxy potatoes

2 eggs

1 tbsp potato flour

salt and freshly ground black pepper

4 tbsp oil

1 Peel the potatoes and grate them into a bowl of cold water. Drain. Squeeze the potato shreds dry in a cloth.

2 Mix the potato with the eggs, flour and seasoning.

3 Heat 1 tbsp of the oil in a frying pan and make your first potato cake using a quarter of the mixture. Spread it out in the pan and flatten it. When the underside is crisp and golden, turn it over and brown the top. Keep it warm while you make the other three.

CHESTNUTS AND VEGETABLES

500 g/1 lb chestnuts

4 tbsp olive oil

2 fat cloves garlic, chopped

175 g/6 oz mushrooms, sliced

340 g/12 oz Brussels sprouts

340 g/12 oz red cabbage

salt and freshly ground black pepper

small glass of red wine

1 Preheat the oven to 200°C/400°F/Gas 6.

2 Make a nick in the top of the chestnuts with a sharp knife and boil them for 10 minutes. Plunge them in cold water and peel.

3 Heat the olive oil in a flameproof casserole and fry the garlic. Add the mushrooms, sprouts and red cabbage and season. Cook, stirring occasionally, for about 5 minutes until coated with oil and beginning to soften.

4 Stir in the chestnuts and red wine. Cover and bake in the oven for 40 minutes. Serve with baked potatoes or a purée of root vegetables (see below).

Chestnuts and vegetables

PUREE OF ROOT VEGETABLES

175 g/6 oz carrots

175 g/6 oz swede (rutabaga)

1 turnip (swede)

1 parsnip

butter

salt and freshly ground black pepper

1 Trim and peel the vegetables and simmer in salted water until tender.

2 Drain and mash to a fluffy purée with butter. Season with salt and plenty of black pepper. Serve with a dish that has a crunchy texture, such as Swiss potato cakes (see p 37), Chestnuts and vegetables (see above) or Nut loaf (see p 47).

FROM THE CUPBOARD

RED-HOT LENTIL SOUP

| 3 tbsp/40 g/1 ½ oz butter |
| 1 large onion, chopped |
| 1 clove garlic, chopped |
| 1 slice fresh ginger, unpeeled |
| 1 slice lemon |
| 1 ⅛ cups/250 g/8 oz red lentils |
| 1.5 l/50 fl oz water |
| salt |
| pinch of paprika |
| 1 green chilli, deseeded and chopped |

1 Heat 2 tbsp/25 g/1 oz butter in a pan and add the onion, garlic, ginger and lemon. Sweat with the lid on over a low heat for 5 minutes.

2 Add the lentils and the water (small red lentils do not need to be presoaked) and season with salt and paprika. Cook for about 40 minutes until lentils have thickened the soup.

3 Heat the remaining butter in a pan and quickly fry the chilli. Serve the soup with chilli topping.

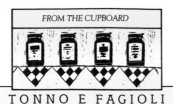
A tasty and nutritious standby meal served with hot pitta bread. You can use cannellini, haricot or butter beans instead of the kidney beans, but the kidney beans look more appealing because of the colour contrast. If you use dried beans, soak overnight, simmer until tender, then drain and allow to cool.

400 g/15 oz can red kidney beans, drained
1 onion chopped
200 g/7 oz can tuna fish
a handful of chopped parsley
a dash of lemon juice
plenty of freshly ground black pepper

1 Mix the beans with the onion. Drain the tuna fish, reserving the oil. Flake and add to the salad.

2 Add the parsley, a dash of lemon juice and plenty of black pepper. Toss and add some of the reserved fish oil and more lemon and pepper to taste.

SAVOURY STUFFED VINE LEAVES

You can buy vine leaves in packets or cans from delicatessens and supermarkets. If you have your own grape vine, pick large, healthy leaves and blanch them in boiling salted water before use.

1 cup/250 g/8 oz brown rice
olive oil
1 small onion, chopped
2 cloves garlic, chopped
salt and freshly ground black pepper
250 g/8 oz chestnuts
1-2 tbsp butter
100 g/4 oz mushrooms
2 tomatoes, peeled and chopped
1 tsp dried mixed herbs
20 vine leaves

1 Wash the rice in several changes of cold water. Heat 1 tbsp oil in a heavy-bottomed pan and fry the onion and garlic until translucent. Stir in the rice and cook for a few minutes before covering with boiling water. (Use about ⅔ water to ⅓ rice by volume.) Bring back to the boil, then cover the pan and turn the heat down very low. The rice should be cooked in about 40 minutes.

2 Meanwhile, prepare the chestnuts (see p 39). Peel and chop them finely.

3 Heat the butter in a pan and add the mushrooms. When they are tender, add the tomatoes, chestnuts and herbs. Stir once or twice and remove from the heat.

4 When the rice is cooked, mix it thoroughly with the nut stuffing and check the seasoning. Use it, by the spoonful, to stuff the vine leaves. Pack them into an ovenproof dish, brush with olive oil and cover the dish with foil. Heat through in the oven. Stuffed vine leaves are best eaten hot, but they're good cold too, if you have any left over.

VEGETARIAN BOLOGNESE SAUCE

Serve as you would a meat Bolognese sauce with pasta. Add 340 g/12 oz wholewheat or spinach pasta shapes to boiling salted water, to which you have added a few drops of oil, and continue boiling for about 9 minutes or until al dente. Toss in the hot sauce and add Parmesan cheese to serve.

1⅛ cups/250 g/8 oz brown lentils
salt and freshly ground black pepper
1 bayleaf
1-2 tbsp olive oil
2 cloves garlic, chopped
1 onion, chopped
1 carrot, chopped
1 stick celery, chopped
400 g/15 oz can tomatoes, mashed
1 tbsp tomato purée (paste)
½ tsp dried mixed herbs
2 tbsp red wine

1 Soak the lentils overnight and simmer in salted water with a bayleaf until they can be mashed with a fork. Drain and discard the bayleaf.

2 Heat the oil in a pan and fry the onions and garlic until translucent. Add the carrot and celery and cook for a further 2 minutes.

3 Add the tomatoes and a little juice. Add the remaining ingredients and the lentils. Simmer until the sauce is quite thick. Blend or part-blend in a blender and serve with pasta.

ROLLMOPS WITH APPLE AND ONIONS

This dressing goes equally well with cold smoked trout if you want a subtler taste.

8 rollmop herrings (rolled herrings)
1 apple
lemon juice
1 large onion
150 ml/5 fl oz soured (sour) cream
2 hardboiled eggs, sliced
sprigs of dill

1 Core the apple, but do not peel. Slice thinly and sprinkle with lemon juice to prevent discolouring. Slice the onion thinly. Mix the apple and onion with the soured cream.

2 Arrange the rollmops on four individual plates with the egg slices to one side. Top the fish with the dressing and decorate with dill. Serve cold with brown bread.

NUT LOAF

1 cup/175 g/6 oz mixed nuts, chopped
1 small aubergine (eggplant)
olive oil
1 large onion, finely chopped
2 cloves garlic, chopped
¾ cup/175 g/6 oz brown rice, cooked (see p 44)
200 g/7 oz can tomatoes, drained and mashed
salt and freshly ground black pepper
2 eggs, beaten

1 Preheat the oven to 190°C/375°F/Gas 5.

2 Put the nuts on a baking (cookie) sheet and toast them at the top of the oven for 10 minutes.

3 Slice the aubergine, sprinkle with salt and leave for 20 minutes. Rinse off the salt, pat dry and dice.

4 Heat 1-2 tbsp oil in a pan. Add the onion and garlic and fry till translucent. Add the aubergine and cook, stirring occasionally, for about 10 minutes. Add more oil as necessary.

5 Transfer the aubergine mixture to a large bowl and stir in the nuts, brown rice and tomatoes. Mix well and season to taste. Stir in the beaten egg.

6 Pour into a greased small loaf pan and smooth the top. Bake in the centre of the oven for 35 minutes until firm. Turn out of the pan and cut into slices to serve.

HOT PASTA SALAD

The dressing	
2 cloves garlic	
3 tbsp olive oil	
a handful of fresh basil leaves	
1 tbsp grated Parmesan cheese	
The salad	
100 g/4 oz Mozzarella cheese	
500 g/1 lb Mediterranean (Italian) tomatoes	
75 g/3 oz black olives	
salt and freshly ground black pepper	
The pasta	
340 g/12 oz spinach pasta twists	
1 tsp olive oil	

1 Chop the garlic and put it in a mortar. Pour in a little of the olive oil and pound it to a pulp. Gradually add the basil leaves and cheese with the rest of the oil, pounding all the time. You should have a thick paste.

2 Dice the Mozzarella. Peel the tomatoes by immersing them in boiling water until their skins burst. Chop them roughly. Mix the cheese, tomatoes and olives together and season.

3 Cook the pasta in boiling salted water, to which you have added a little olive oil, until *al dente*. Drain. Toss the pasta in the dressing. Pile it into four warmed serving bowls and top with the salad.

Hot pasta salad

SPAGHETTI MASCARPONE

Mascarpone is an Italian cheese sold in muslin bags. You can substitute cream cheese if you can't get the real thing. This dish takes only minutes to prepare. The secret is not to overcook the eggs – the sauce should be only just starting to set when you toss in the spaghetti.

340 g/12 oz wholewheat spaghetti
salt and freshly ground black pepper
a little oil
100 g/4 oz Mascarpone cheese
2 egg yolks
grated Parmesan cheese to serve

1 Cook the pasta in boiling salted water, to which you have added a few drops of oil, until *al dente*.

2 While you are draining the spaghetti, stir the egg yolks and Mascarpone together in a large pan over a low heat.

3 When the sauce begins to set, toss in the spaghetti. Serve at once with plenty of black pepper and Parmesan. This dish should be accompanied by a crunchy salad.

TAGLIATELLE (NOODLES) WITH SWEET PEPPER SAUCE

350 g/12 oz spinach tagliatelle (noodles)
2 tsp oil
½ tsp salt
The sauce
1 small firm red pepper (capsicum)
1 small green pepper
1 small yellow pepper
1-2 tbsp olive oil
1 onion, chopped
2 cloves garlic, chopped
400 g/15 oz can tomatoes
1 tbsp tomato purée (paste)
fresh basil leaves, snipped
salt and freshly ground black pepper

1 Trim and deseed the peppers and cut into narrow strips. You can make the sauce with green peppers alone if you wish, but the red and yellow varieties are sweeter and make the dish look more colourful. Blanch the peppers for a minute in boiling salted water, refresh in cold water, then drain.

2 Heat the olive oil in a pan, add the garlic and onions and cook gently, stirring, until soft. Add the tomatoes, tomato purée and basil. Break up the tomatoes with a wooden spoon and simmer for about 5 minutes. Season to taste and blend the sauce in a blender. Return to the pan over a very low heat and add the peppers.

3 Cook the pasta in a large pan with plenty of water to which you have added a little oil and the salt. The water should be at a full rolling boil. The pasta will be ready in about 9 minutes. Drain and divide between individual warmed serving bowls.

4 Spoon the sauce over each helping of pasta and serve at once with Parmesan cheese.

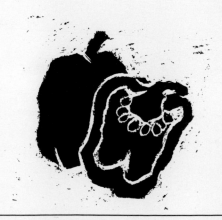

CORN CROQUETTES

3 tbsp butter
3 tbsp flour
300 ml/10 fl oz milk
salt and freshly ground black pepper
1-2 tbsp finely chopped parsley
2⅓ cups/400 g/14 oz corn kernels, cooked
2 egg yolks
The coating
2 eggs, beaten
seasoned flour
fine stale breadcrumbs
oil for frying

1 To make the sauce, cut the butter into small pieces and melt in a heavy-bottomed pan. Stir in the flour and cook for a few minutes until the mixture is a pale gold.

2 Remove from the heat and pour in the milk. Stir well, return to the heat and stir until the sauce has thickened. Season with salt and plenty of pepper.

3 Stir the parsley, corn kernels and egg yolks into the mixture. Chill.

4 The mixture should have a heavy dropping consistency. Form it into croquettes. Dip in the beaten egg, then roll in the flour and breadcrumbs, coating each croquette finely.

5 Fry the croquettes in oil until heated through and crisp on the outside.

FLAGEOLET AND SAGE DERBY QUICHE

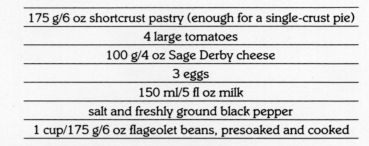

175 g/6 oz shortcrust pastry (enough for a single-crust pie)
4 large tomatoes
100 g/4 oz Sage Derby cheese
3 eggs
150 ml/5 fl oz milk
salt and freshly ground black pepper
1 cup/175 g/6 oz flageolet beans, presoaked and cooked

1 Preheat the oven to 200°C/400°F/Gas 6.

2 Pour boiling water over the tomatoes. After a minute the skins will begin to split. Refresh with cold water. Peel the tomatoes and slice them thickly.

3 Line a 22-cm (8-in) quiche pan with the pastry and crumble the cheese into it. Arrange the tomato slices to cover the cheese.

4 Break the eggs into a bowl and lightly beat with the milk and seasoning. Pour egg mixture into the pie crust, gently pressing down the tomatoes with a fork.

5 Bake in the centre of the oven for 15-20 minutes, until set and golden.

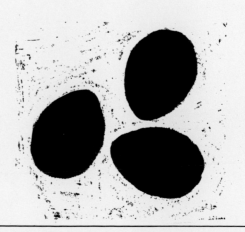

SALMON MOUSSE

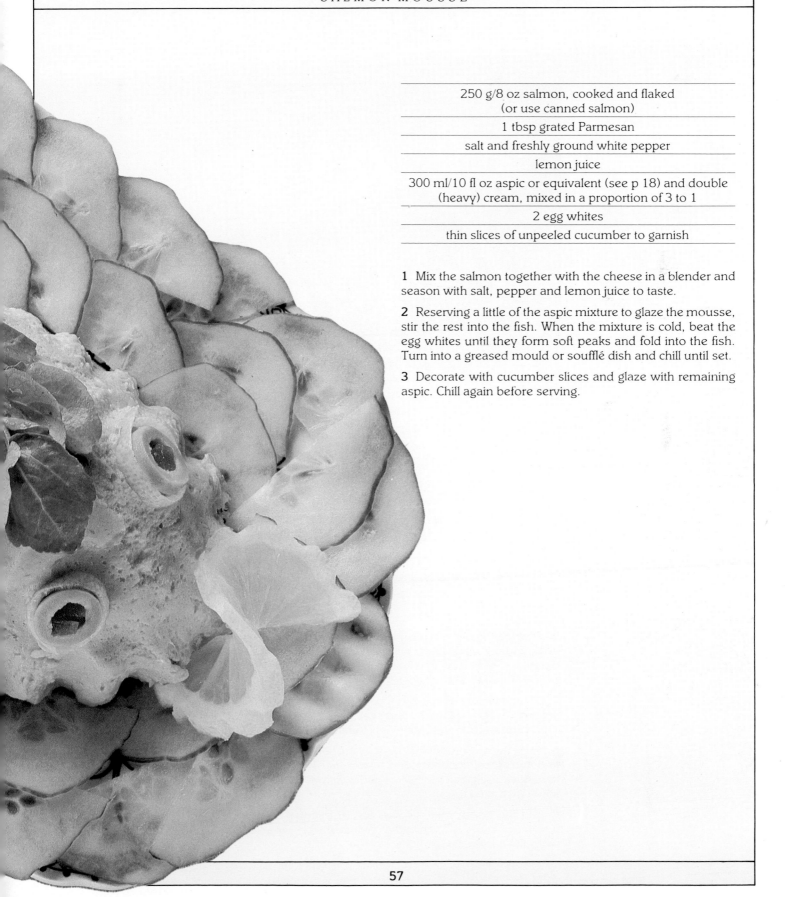

| 250 g/8 oz salmon, cooked and flaked (or use canned salmon) |
| 1 tbsp grated Parmesan |
| salt and freshly ground white pepper |
| lemon juice |
| 300 ml/10 fl oz aspic or equivalent (see p 18) and double (heavy) cream, mixed in a proportion of 3 to 1 |
| 2 egg whites |
| thin slices of unpeeled cucumber to garnish |

1 Mix the salmon together with the cheese in a blender and season with salt, pepper and lemon juice to taste.

2 Reserving a little of the aspic mixture to glaze the mousse, stir the rest into the fish. When the mixture is cold, beat the egg whites until they form soft peaks and fold into the fish. Turn into a greased mould or soufflé dish and chill until set.

3 Decorate with cucumber slices and glaze with remaining aspic. Chill again before serving.

175 g/6 oz rose cocoa beans
2 tbsp olive oil
½ tsp fennel seeds
½ tsp mustard seeds
1 onion, chopped
2 cloves garlic, chopped
100 g/4 oz mushrooms, sliced
½ fresh green chilli, deseeded and chopped
400 g/15 oz can tomatoes, mashed
2 tbsp chopped fresh coriander (cilantro) or parsley
salt and freshly ground black pepper

1 Soak the beans overnight and cook them in salted water until tender. Cooking time will vary depending on the age of the beans. They could be ready in 20 minutes, or they may take an hour, so keep testing.

2 Meanwhile, heat the oil in a pan and, when hot, add the seeds. As soon as the mustard seeds begin to pop, add the onion and garlic. Cook gently until translucent.

3 Stir in the mushrooms. When they are tender, add the chilli and tomatoes, coriander and seasoning. If you can't get coriander, use parsley instead, but the dish will certainly lose some of its character.

4 Add the beans, heat through for 10 minutes and serve with thick slices of wholemeal (wholewheat) bread for a warming winter supper.

TUNA AND TOMATO CHEESECAKE

To make a fish cheesecake, follow the recipe for Broccoli and tomato cheesecake on p 24, but replace the broccoli with 200 g/7 oz canned tuna fish and season with cayenne pepper and lemon juice instead of nutmeg. Decorate the top with thin overlapping slices of tomato and brush with gelatine if you wish. Chill before serving.

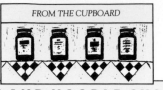

PRUNE AND NOODLE CUSTARD

1 cup/175 g/6 oz dried prunes
250 g/8 oz wholewheat macaroni
3 eggs
300 ml/10 fl oz milk
2 tbsp honey
1 tsp vanilla extract
pinch of nutmeg

1 Pour boiling water over the prunes and leave to plump up overnight.

2 Preheat the oven to 160°C/375°F/Gas 3.

3 Cook the macaroni in boiling salted water, to which you have added a few drops of oil, until tender.

4 In a bowl, beat together the eggs, milk, honey and vanilla with a fork.

5 Grease an ovenproof casserole and mix the prunes and noodles together in it. Pour over the custard and sprinkle the top with nutmeg. Bake for half an hour and serve hot. This dish also tastes good chilled.

FROM THE GRANARY

WHOLEMEAL (WHOLEWHEAT) BREAD

Makes 2 large loaves
2 packages/25 g/1 oz dried yeast *or* 50 g/2 oz fresh yeast
600 ml/20 fl oz warm water
1 tsp molasses
2 tbsp malt extract
2 tbsp olive oil
2 tbsp salt
7½-8 cups/1 kg/2 lbs wholewheat flour

1 Preheat the oven to 230°C/450°F/Gas 8. Put the yeast in a small bowl and pour some of the water over it. Stir in the molasses and leave in a warm place for 10 minutes. The yeast will usually form a froth, but don't worry if it doesn't.

2 Meanwhile, stir the malt extract, olive oil and salt into the rest of the water.

3 In a large bowl, combine the flour with the yeasty liquid and enough of the water to make a dough. You may not need all the water as some flours absorb more than others do.

4 On a floured surface, knead the dough for about 7 minutes. Put it in an oiled polythene (plastic) bag in a warm place to rise for an hour.

5 Knead the dough again for 1 minute. Divide it into two and place each half in an oiled loaf pan 22×12 cm (8½×4½ in). Cover the pans with a clean damp cloth and put them on top of the stove for 20 minutes.

6 Bake in the centre of the oven for 10 minutes and then turn the heat down to 190°C/375°F/Gas 5 and bake for a further 25 minutes. Turn the loaves out of the pans and return them to the oven for 5 minutes to crisp the crust. Allow to cool on a wire rack.

WALNUT BREAD

For a very good flavoursome loaf with added texture, add ½ cup/50 g/2 oz roughly chopped walnuts to the flour and use walnut oil instead of olive oil. Omit the molasses. This loaf will fill the kitchen with its delicious nutty aroma and taste marvellous with jam for breakfast. Or try Cheddar and watercress sandwiches in walnut bread with tomato soup for supper.

Walnut bread

MARMITE BREAD

For a tangy savoury loaf, omit the molasses and replace the malt extract with Marmite (yeast extract spread). Add 1-2 tbsp caraway seeds to the flour and sprinkle the top of the loaf with the seeds, too. This bread is good with strong Cheddar or simply with butter as an accompaniment to a lunchtime bowl of soup.

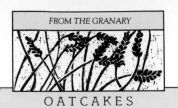
OATCAKES

Makes about 22

½ cup/100 g/4 oz soft brown sugar

½ cups/50 g/2 oz plain untreated (all-purpose) flour

1 cup/100 g/4 oz wheatmeal (wholewheat) flour

1⅓ cup/100 g/4 oz porridge (rolled) oats

pinch of bicarbonate of (baking) soda

pinch of salt

8 tbsp/100 g/4 oz butter

1 egg yolk

1 Preheat the oven to 180°C/350°F/Gas 4.

2 Mix the dry ingredients together in a bowl. Cut the butter into small pieces in the bowl and rub in with the fingertips.

3 Mix in the egg yolk and form into a dough. Knead for a few minutes and then roll out thinly on a lightly floured surface and cut into rounds with a biscuit cutter.

4 Leaving plenty of space between each one, arrange the rounds on a greased baking (cookie) sheet and bake for 10-15 minutes until crisp and golden. Allow to cool slightly before transferring to a wire rack. When cool, store in an airtight tin. Serve with cheese.

AMARETTI (ALMOND BISCUITS OR COOKIES)

Makes about 20

2 egg whites

½ cup/100 g/4 oz fruit sugar (fructose)

⅔ cup/100 g/4 oz ground almonds

1 tsp kirsch (optional)

a few drops vanilla essence (extract)

almond slivers for decorating

1 Preheat the oven to 180°C/350°F/Gas 4.

2 Whisk the egg whites until they form soft peaks. Gradually add the sugar, whisking continuously until the mixture is thick and lustrous. Stir in the ground almonds, kirsch and vanilla essence.

3 Line baking (cookie) sheets with sheets of rice paper. Take a spoonful of mixture about the size of a plum and roll it into a ball in the palms of your hands. With a sticky mixture, you will find it easier if your hands are wet. Flatten the balls and arrange them on the baking trays with plenty of space for them to expand during cooking.

4 Decorate each biscuit with a sliver of almond and bake for 20-30 minutes. Allow to cool slightly, then carefully remove biscuits with their rice paper bases (which are edible) and cool them completely on a wire rack. Store in a tin and serve with stewed fruit or ice cream.

BRAN AND SULTANA (RAISIN) MUFFINS

Makes 12
2 tbsp oil
2 tbsp honey
1 egg
150 ml/5 fl oz milk
1¼ cups/125 g/5 oz wholewheat flour
75 g/3 oz bran
2 tsp baking powder
pinch of salt
⅓ cup/50 g/2 oz sultanas (seedless, white raisins)

1 Preheat the oven to 190°C/375°F/Gas 5.

2 Beat together the oil and honey. Beat in the egg. Gradually beat in the milk until smooth.

3 Combine the dry ingredients and stir these into the liquid ones. When the bran has soaked up the liquid, you should have a soft dough.

4 Spoon into an oiled muffin tin and bake for about 20 minutes.

SPICED BUTTERMILK SCONES (BISCUITS)

Makes 8
2 cups/250 g/8 oz plain untreated (all-purpose) flour
2 cups/250 g/8 oz wholewheat flour
2 tsp bicarbonate of (baking) soda
2 tsp cream of tartar
1 tbsp fruit sugar (fructose)
1 tsp mixed spice
8 tbsp/100 g/4 oz butter
300 ml/10 fl oz buttermilk
3 tsp baking powder

1 Preheat the oven to 220°C/425°F/Gas 7.

2 Sift the flours together and mix thoroughly with the other dry ingredients. Cut the butter into the flour mix and rub in well with the fingertips.

3 Stir in the buttermilk and mix to form a soft dough. Knead the dough lightly on a floured board. Divide in half, form each half into a round and cut each round into four wedges. Place the wedges on a greased baking (cookie) sheet, dust with flour and bake for about 12 minutes.

4 Cool on a wire rack. Best eaten while still warm. Slice them in half and fill with butter and jam, or jam and clotted cream.

SESAME SNAPS

Makes about 20

1 cup/100 g/4 oz wholewheat flour

½ cup/50 g/2 oz sesame seeds

1 tsp baking powder

1-2 tsp salt

2 tsp tahini (sesame) paste

1 tbsp olive oil

2-3 fl oz tepid water

1 Preheat the oven to 220°C/425°F/Gas 7.

2 Combine the dry ingredients in a bowl. Add the tahini paste and olive oil and mix with the fingertips until crumbly. Gradually add enough water to form a soft dough.

3 Knead gently on a floured board and then roll out thinly. Press out rounds with a biscuit cutter and arrange on a greased baking (cookie) sheet. Bake in the oven for 15 minutes until crisp and golden.

4 Cool on a wire rack, store in a tin and serve with cheese.

HAZELNUT AND APRICOT CRUNCH

Makes about 16 bars

8 tbsp/100 g/4 oz butter

⅓ cup/50 g/2 oz soft brown sugar

2 tbsp maple syrup

1⅓ cups/100 g/4 oz porridge (rolled) oats

½ cup/50 g/2 oz chopped hazelnuts

⅓ cup/50 g/2 oz dried apricots, chopped

1 Preheat the oven to 180°/350°F/Gas 4.

2 Put the butter, sugar and syrup in a heavy-bottomed pan and stir over a low heat until combined.

3 Stir in the remaining ingredients. Press into a Swiss (jelly) roll pan lined with greased parchment or greaseproof paper.

4 Bake for about 45 minutes, until golden. Cut into bars in the pan using an oiled knife. Cool in the tin.

PIZZA

The dough

12 g/½ oz fresh yeast (or ½ package/6 g/¼ oz dried yeast)
150 ml/5 fl oz warm water
1½ cups/175 g/6 oz wholewheat flour (or half wholewheat and half plain untreated [all-purpose] flour)
½ tsp salt
4 tbsp olive oil

1 Preheat the oven to 220°C/425°F/Gas 7.

2 Put the yeast and water in a bowl in a warm place for about 10 minutes. It will probably froth up, but don't worry if it doesn't. Your pizza will still work.

3 Sift the flour with the salt into a warm bowl. Make a well in the middle and pour in the yeast mixture and the olive oil.

4 Mix together well and knead on a floured board for about 5 minutes. Put the dough in an oiled polythene (plastic) bag and leave in a warm place to rise for an hour.

5 In the meantime, prepare your topping (see below).

6 Knock back the dough and knead it for another minute or two. This quantity of dough will make two 22-cm (8-in) pizzas; one is enough for a main meal for one person. Or you may prefer to make several smaller pizzas. Divide the dough accordingly and roll it out. Place the pizzas on a greased baking (cookie) sheet and crimp the edges slightly to stop the topping from running over the sides. Spread with the topping.

7 Bake for about 20-25 minutes. Pizzas are best served straight away.

Tomato

2-3 tbsp olive oil
2 onions, chopped
2 cloves garlic, chopped
2 tsp oregano or marjoram
salt and freshly ground black papper
400 g/ 15 oz ripe tomatoes, peeled (or use canned)
100 g/ 4 oz Mozzarella cheese

1 Heat the oil in a pan and add the onion and garlic. Cook gently until translucent.

2 Add the tomatoes, breaking them up with a wooden spoon. Stir in the herbs and season well. Cook the sauce gently for about 20 minutes until thick. For a smoother sauce, purée in the blender or food processor.

3 Pour the sauce onto the pizzas and top with slices of Mozzarella cheese.

Mushroom

5 tbsp olive oil
2-3 cloves garlic, crushed
500 g/1 lb mushrooms, sliced
a handful of chopped parsley
salt and freshly ground black pepper

1 Heat the olive oil in a pan and cook the garlic until translucent.

2 Add the mushrooms and cook gently, stirring, until very black and juicy.

3 Add the parsley and stir till it has absorbed the juice. Season with salt and plenty of black pepper and spoon on to the pizzas.

Sardine

tomato topping (as above)
6 fresh sardines or 2 cans, drained
10 black olives, pitted
100 g/4 oz Mozzarella cheese

1 Pour half the sauce onto the pizzas. Clean and halve the sardines if fresh. Arrange the fish and olives on the sauce and cover with the remaining tomato sauce.

2 Top with thin slices of Mozzarella.

Mussel

500 g/20 fl oz mussels
3 tbsp/40 g/1 1/2 oz butter
1 small onion, chopped
1 glass white wine
a handful of parsley
tomato topping (as above)
250 g/8 oz Mozzarella cheese

1 Prepare the mussels. Remove the beards and scrub the shells well. Rinse in running water. Discard any broken or open shells.

2 Heat the butter in a large saucepan and, when melted, stir in the onion. Add the mussels, white wine, water and parsley. Bring to the boil and then turn the heat down and cover the pan. Steam the mussels until the shells have opened.

3 Remove mussels from their shells. Add some of the cooking liquor to the tomato topping and cook to reduce.

4 Spoon half of the tomato mixture onto the pizzas. Arrange the mussels on top of it and cover with the rest of the tomato. Top with slices of Mozzarella cheese.

STUFFED PANCAKES

Makes 9 small pancakes

The pancakes

⅜ cup/40 g/1½ oz plain untreated (all-purpose) flour

⅜ cup/40 g/1½ oz wholewheat flour

pinch of salt

1 egg

150 ml/5 fl oz milk

1 tbsp melted butter

Cheese and herb filling

2 cups/500 g/1 lb curd (cottage) cheese

2 tbsp cream

1 fat clove garlic, crushed

2 tbsp finely chopped fresh herbs

1 tbsp chopped spring onion (scallion)

1 To make the pancake batter, sift the flour and salt into a bowl. Make a well in the middle of it and add the egg.

2 Gradually beat in the milk. When half of the milk has been added, beat in the melted butter. Continue beating in the milk until you have a thin batter. Allow the batter to stand for half an hour.

3 Meanwhile, prepare the filling. Combine the curd cheese with the rest of the ingredients and mix well.

4 To make the pancakes, oil a heavy-bottomed frying pan 18 cm (7 in) in diameter. Place it on the flame and when it is very hot, add 2 tbsp of the batter. Tilt the pan so that the batter covers the base. Cook until the pancake is beginning to brown on the underside and then turn over and cook the top. You may have to throw the first pancake away, as it will absorb the excess oil in the pan.

5 Continue making pancakes, keeping them warm, until all the batter is used up. Divide the filling between them, rolling the pancakes around it into a cigar shape.

6 Arrange the stuffed pancakes in an ovenproof dish and heat in a moderate oven, or microwave, for 1½ minutes.

Smoked salmon and cheese filling

As an alternative to the herbs, add 100 g/4 oz smoked salmon, snipped into small pieces with a pair of scissors, to the cheese and season with cayenne pepper. It is better to use curd cheese with the addition of a little cream for these recipes than it is to use cream cheese, as this tends to curdle when cooked.

FROM THE SEA AND RIVERS

Fish Soup *82*

Cod Steaks in Creamy Tomato Sauce *84*

Scandinavian Fish Pudding *85*

Trout with Orange and Red Pepper (Capsicum) *87*

Prawns (Shrimp) St Jacques *88*

Crab and Asparagus Tart *89*

Fried Prawns (Shrimps) with Cauliflower and Mangetouts
(Snow Peas) *90*

FISH SOUP

4 tbsp olive oil

2 onions, chopped

3 cloves of garlic, crushed

¼ fennel bulb, chopped

2 Mediterranean (Italian) tomatoes

1 kg/2 lb mixed white fish, cleaned and skinned

2 tsp turmeric

salt and freshly ground black pepper

9 cups water

Parmesan cheese to serve

1 Heat the olive oil in a large pan and add the onions, garlic and fennel. Cover the pan, lower the heat and sweat, stirring occasionally, until the vegetables are soft.

2 Meanwhile, skin the tomatoes by first pouring boiling water over them. After a minute, the skins should burst. Refresh the tomatoes in cold water, remove the skins, chop the flesh and discard the seeds.

3 Dust the fish with turmeric and add it with the tomatoes to the vegetables. Cook, stirring, for a few minutes.

4 Add the remaining ingredients. Heat the soup gently until just under the boiling point. Skim off anything that floats to the top. Turn the heat down and cook gently for 20-30 minutes. Serve hot with crusty bread and Parmesan cheese.

COD STEAKS IN CREAMY TOMATO SAUCE

1-2 tbsp olive oil
1 onion, finely chopped
1 clove garlic, finely chopped
1 stick celery, finely chopped
2 large tomatoes, skinned and deseeded, or 4 canned tomatoes
4 cod steaks
salt and freshly ground black pepper
150 ml/5 fl oz dry white wine
150 ml/5 fl oz fish stock
1 tsp cornflour (cornstarch)
2 tbsp single (light) cream
4 sprigs of dill

1 Preheat the oven to 220°C/425°F/Gas 7.

2 Heat the oil in a pan and add the onion, garlic and celery. Cook until soft. Add the tomatoes and cook, stirring, for a few minutes.

3 Transfer the vegetables to an ovenproof dish and lay the fish steaks on top. Season the fish and then pour the wine and fish stock over it. (You can make a good fish stock very easily by simmering offcuts (trimmings) of mixed fish in water to which you have added half a carrot, a small onion and a bayleaf.) Cover and cook in the oven for 20 minutes.

4 Carefully lift out the fish and place on warmed individual plates. Keep hot. Blend the sauce in a blender and pour into a small heavy-bottomed pan. Blend the cornflour with 1 tbsp warm water and stir into the sauce. Bring to the boil, stirring continuously. Remove from the heat and stir in the cream.

5 Pour the sauce decoratively over and around the fish and garnish each steak with a sprig of dill.

SCANDINAVIAN FISH PUDDING

Serves 6

1 kg/2 lb cod or haddock fillets, skinned, but with skins reserved
salt and freshly ground black pepper
2 tbsp potato flour
4 tbsp/50 g/2 oz butter, softened
300 ml/10 fl oz single (light) cream
1 tbsp olive oil
50 g/2 oz mushrooms
whole prawns (shrimp) and lumpfish roe to garnish

1 Preheat the oven to 200°C/400°F/Gas 6.

2 Chop the fish and pound in the seasoning and flour until you have a thick paste. Beat in the butter and cream.

3 Heat the olive oil in a pan and gently sauté the mushrooms. Stir these carefully into the mixture.

4 Spoon the mixture into a greased ovenproof oblong dish and smooth the top. Cover and stand in a roasting tin of simmering water for an hour.

5 Turn the pudding out onto a plate and cut it into thick slices. Transfer the slices to individual plates and serve hot or cold, garnished with prawns and lumpfish roe.

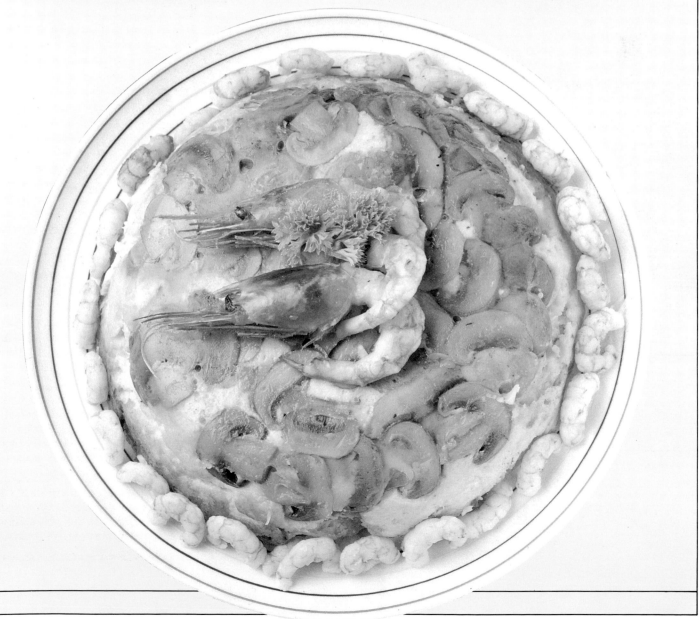

TROUT WITH ORANGE AND RED PEPPER (CAPSICUM)

4 trout
salt and freshly ground black pepper
2 oranges
1 red pepper (capsicum)
2 tbsp olive oil
2 egg yolks
150 ml/5 fl oz dry white wine
2 tbsp/25 g/1 oz butter, softened

1 Wash the trout, pat dry and season. Place in a shallow dish and squeeze the juice from 1½ of the oranges over it. Slice the remaining ½ orange into slivers and set aside. Leave the fish to marinate for 30 minutes.

2 Slice and deseed the red pepper and blanch in boiling water for 1 minute. Refresh under cold water, then drain.

3 Reserving the marinade, brush the fish with oil, then grill gently until tender (about 5 minutes each side).

4 Mix together the marinade, wine and egg yolks. Pour into a double boiler and stir over boiling water until the sauce has thickened. Beat in the butter and stir in the red pepper.

5 Arrange the trout on a serving dish, pour the sauce over it and garnish with orange slivers.

PRAWNS (SHRIMP) ST JACQUES

500 g/1 lb potatoes, peeled
butter
salt and freshly ground black pepper
500 g/1 lb prawns (shrimp)
The sauce
2 tbsp/12 g/1 oz butter
¼ cup/12 g/1 oz plain untreated (all-purpose) flour
150 ml/5 fl oz milk
150 ml/5 fl oz cream
12 g/1 oz Parmesan cheese
The topping
grated Parmesan cheese
breadcrumbs
chopped parsley

1 Boil the potatoes in salted water until they can be pierced with a knife. Mash them with the butter and salt and pepper to taste. Peel the prawns.

2 Make the sauce. Melt the butter in a pan and stir in the flour. Cook, stirring, for a few minutes and then gradually stir in the milk. Add the cream and cheese and season. Add the prawns.

3 Pipe the potato round the edge of 4 scallop shells. Fill with the prawn sauce and sprinkle with Parmesan, breadcrumbs and chopped parsley. Brown lightly under the grill and serve hot.

FROM THE SEA AND RIVERS

CRAB AND ASPARAGUS TART

175 g/6 oz pastry (enough for a single-crust pie)

2 eggs plus 1 yolk

150 ml/5 fl oz double (heavy) cream

1 tbsp brandy

250 g/8 oz crabmeat

2 tbsp/25 g/1 oz butter

¼ cup/25 g/1 oz flour

150 ml/5 fl oz milk

2 tbsp grated Cheddar cheese

salt and cayenne pepper

8 asparagus spears, cooked

1 Preheat the oven to 190°C/375°F/Gas 5.

2 Roll out the pastry and line a 22-cm (8-in) quiche ring standing on a greased baking (cookie) sheet.

3 Beat the eggs, cream and brandy together. Flake the crabmeat with a fork and stir into the egg mixture.

4 Melt the butter in a heavy-bottomed pan and add the flour. Stir and cook for a few minutes. Remove from the heat and gradually stir in the milk. Return to the heat and continue stirring until the sauce thickens. Add the cheese and seasoning.

5 Stir the crab mixture into the cheese sauce and pour into the flan. Decorate the top with asparagus spears, pushing them into the filling. Bake for 35-40 minutes till lightly set.

FRIED PRAWNS (SHRIMPS) WITH CAULIFLOWER AND MANGETOUTS (SNOW PEAS)

Serves 2
100 g/4 oz prawns, shelled
The marinade
2 tsp egg white
½ tsp sherry
1 tsp cornflour (cornstarch)
pinch of salt
oil
50 g/2 oz cauliflower florets
50 g/2 oz mangetouts (snow peas)
2 slices ginger
2 tsp chopped onion
The sauce
1 tsp sherry
½ tsp sesame oil
salt and freshly ground white pepper
chopped chives for garnish

1 Marinate the prawns for 20 minutes.

2 Heat 3 tbsp oil in a pan and fry the cauliflower florets for about 4 minutes. For the last 30 seconds, add the prawns and mangetouts. Drain well.

3 Heat 1 tbsp oil and fry the onion and ginger for 10 seconds. Add the prawns and vegetables and fry for a further 30 seconds. Add the sauce ingredients and stir once. Garnish with chives and serve with boiled rice.

FROM THE ORCHARD & HEDGEROW

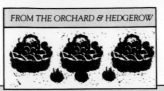

CHERRY SOUP

500 g/1 lb cherries

900 ml/30 fl oz water

juice of half a lemon

honey to taste

ground cinnamon

soured (sour) cream to serve

1 Simmer the cherries in the water with the lemon juice until soft. With a slotted spoon, remove. Discard the stones.

2 Blend the soup in a blender and add honey and a pinch of ground cinnamon to taste.

3 Allow to cool, then chill in the fridge. Serve with a swirl of soured cream.

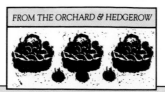

CREAM OF NETTLE SOUP

1 kg/2 lb young nettles
2 tbsp/25 g/1 oz butter
1 small onion, chopped
¼ cup/25 g/1 oz flour
900 ml/30 fl oz milk
salt and freshly ground black pepper
2 egg yolks
1 tbsp single (light) cream
cream and croûtons to serve

1 Pick the young nettle leaves before the plants flower. Discard the stalks, wash the leaves and press them into a pan with only the water that is clinging to them. Cover the pan and cook until soft (5-8 minutes). Purée in a blender.

2 Heat the butter in a pan and cook the onion until soft. Stir in the flour. Stir in a little milk and cook until thick. Stir in enough of the remaining milk to make a very thin sauce. Add the milk and the sauce to the nettles. Season well.

3 Beat the egg yolks with the cream. Stir in a little of the soup, then return to the pan. Heat through and check seasoning.

4 To serve, add a swirl of cream and some croûtons to each individual bowl.

ELDERFLOWER WATER ICE

A water ice like this refreshes the palate between courses. It can also be served as a very light dessert.

600 ml/20 fl oz water
1 cup/250 g/8 oz fruit sugar (fructose)
6 heads elderflowers
juice of 1 lemon
2 egg whites

1 Heat the water and add the sugar, stirring until dissolved. Add the elderflowers and lemon juice and bring to the boil.

2 Strain the syrup through a jelly bag. Allow it to cool, then freeze.

3 When the syrup is half frozen, beat the egg whites until stiff and fold into the syrup. Freeze in individual dishes.

BUCKWHEAT PANCAKES WITH BILBERRY (BLUEBERRY) FILLING

The bilberry is a knee-high shrub that grows abundantly on heaths and moorland. The fruit is small, round, black and juicy and can be gathered from midsummer onwards. The bilberry is sparse-fruiting and so takes a long time to pick. Blackberries can be used as an alternative in this recipe.

Makes 9 small pancakes
The pancakes
⅜ cup/40 g/1½ oz wholewheat flour
⅛ cup/40 g/1½ oz buckwheat flour
pinch of salt
1 egg
150 ml/5 fl oz milk
1 tbsp melted butter
The filling
500 g/1 lb bilberries (blueberries)
4 tbsp honey
whipped cream to serve

1 To make the pancake batter, sift the flour and salt into a bowl. Make a well in the middle of it and add the egg.

2 Gradually beat in the milk. When half of the milk has been added, beat in the melted butter. Continue beating in the milk until you have a thin batter. Allow the batter to stand for half an hour.

3 Meanwhile, prepare the filling. Wash and pick over the bilberries. Put them in a heavy-bottomed pan over a very low flame. It is best to add no water at all. When the fruit is submerged in its own juice, add the honey and stir until dissolved. The syrup should be thick and fruity.

4 To make the pancakes, oil a heavy-bottomed pan 18 cm (7 in) in diameter. Place it on the flame and when it is very hot, add 2 tbsp of the batter. Tilt the pan so that the batter covers the base. Cook until the pancake is beginning to brown on the underside and then turn over and cook the other side. You may have to throw the first pancake away, as it will absorb the excess oil in the pan.

5 Continue making pancakes, keeping them warm, until all the batter has been used up. Divide the filling between them and roll the pancakes into cigar shapes.

6 Serve each pancake with a dollop of whipped cream.

Buckwheat pancakes with bilberry (bluberry) filling

GREEN BEECH LIQUEUR

tender young beech leaves

vodka

fruit sugar (fructose)

brandy

1 Pick young beech leaves in late spring or early summer. Make sure they are tender. (What you don't use in this recipe you can eat in a salad).

2 Pack the leaves into a jar and press them well down. Fill the jar with vodka. Seal and leave for two weeks in a dark place.

3 Strain off the vodka, which will now be a bright green in colour.

4 To make the liqueur, prepare a syrup of 1 cup/250 g/8 oz fruit sugar and 300 ml/10 fl oz boiling water to every pint of vodka. Stir the sugar into the water until dissolved. When cool, add 1 tbsp brandy for each 10 fl oz of water and sugar and combine with the vodka. Bottle and seal.

ripe sloes

the best Dutch gin

Sloes are the blue-black fruit of the blackthorn bush and can be harvested in October. Pick over them and remove the stalks.

1 Half fill a bottle with sloes and fill it to the top with gin. Seal the bottle and store in a dark place.

2 The gin will take on a beautiful pink colour and a tangy fruity flavour within about two weeks. You can leave it longer if you want a stronger, fruitier taste, or you can decant the gin and top up the bottle with fresh gin a second time. Sloe gin makes an ideal Christmas drink.

RASPBERRY ICE CREAM

1 cup raspberries

1 tbsp dried milk powder

2 tbsp yogurt

2 tbsp honey

250 ml/9 fl oz whipping cream

1 Purée the raspberries with the milk powder, yogurt and honey in a blender. Freeze.

2 When the raspberries have frozen into a mush, whip the cream and mix in well. Return to the freezer. Serve with Amaretti (see p 69).

Raspberry ice cream

PEAR SOUFFLE

500 g/1 lb pears	
1-2 tbsp butter	
a little honey	
a pinch of cinnamon	
3 large eggs, separated	
butter to coat the dish	

1 Preheat the oven to 200°C/400°F/Gas 6.

2 Peel, halve and core the pears. Cut them into slices.

3 Heat the butter in a pan and add the pear slices. When the fruit has softened, raise the heat a little, break up the fruit with a wooden spoon and cook till mushy.

4 Put the contents of the pan into a blender. Blend until smooth and add a little honey and cinnamon to taste. Pour into a bowl and beat in the egg yolks.

5 Butter a 1.75-l/60-fl oz soufflé dish. Whisk the egg whites until they form soft peaks and fold into the mixture. Pour into the soufflé dish and bake in the oven for 20-25 minutes until just golden brown and nearly set.

FRENCH APPLE TART

The pastry

¾ cup/75 g/3 oz plain untreated (all-purpose) flour

¾ cup/75 g/3 oz wholewheat flour

⅓ cup/50 g/2 oz ground almonds

8 tbsp/100 g/4 oz butter, softened

1 egg

¼ cup/50 g/2 oz fruit sugar (fructose)

pinch of salt

The filling

6 cooking apples

10 tbsp/150 g/5 oz butter

2-3 tbsp fruit sugar (fructose)

2 tsp mixed splice

1 Preheat the oven to 200°C/400°F/Gas 6.

2 To make the pastry, sift the flours and almonds together onto a board and make a well in the middle. Put the remaining ingredients into the well and work in with your fingertips until you have a smooth dough. Knead for a few minutes, then leave for half an hour in the fridge.

3 Meanwhile, peel, core and slice the apples. Heat the butter in a pan and fry the apples gently until soft and golden.

4 Add the sugar and spice and continue to cook, stirring, until the apple is coated with syrup.

5 Line a greased 22-cm (8-in) loose-bottomed quiche pan with the pastry and fill with the apple. Bake for 25-30 minutes and serve with whipped cream.

FROM THE DAIRY

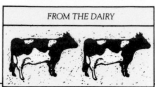

DOUBLE GLOUCESTER SALAD

Serves 2
100 g/4 oz Double Gloucester cheese
1 bunch watercress
2 handfuls young spinach leaves
2 large Mediterranean (Italian) tomatoes
50 g/2 oz mushrooms
6-8 spring onions (scallions)
2 tbsp olive oil
1 tbsp wine vinegar
1-2 tsp mustard powder
salt and freshly ground black pepper

1 Cube the cheese. Wash the spinach and watercress, discarding stalks and any tough or yellow leaves. Immerse the tomatoes in boiling water until their skins split, then refresh with cold water, peel and roughly chop. Slice the mushrooms. Trim the spring onions; make several lengthwise cuts around each into the onion and splay out the layers in a decorative fashion.

2 Make the dressing by combining the oil, vinegar, mustard and seasoning.

3 Combine the watercress, spinach, tomatoes and mushrooms in a salad bowl, add the dressing and toss. Top with the cheese and onions.

Double Gloucester salad

MOZARRELLA AND AVOCADO BEES

Serves 2
1 ripe avocado
100 g/4 oz Mozzarella cheese
1 tbsp olive oil
1 tbsp tarragon vinegar
salt and freshly ground black pepper

1 Cut the avocado in half and remove the stone. With a palette knife (spatula) carefully remove the flesh from each half of the avocado in one piece.

2 Lay the avocado halves flat-side downwards and cut horizontally into 1-cm (¼-inch) slides.

3 Cut semi-circular slices of the same width from the Mozzarella, with 4 extra semi-circles for wings.

4 Arrange the cheese slices between the avocado slices to form the striped body of the bee, and arrange the wings at the sides.

5 Mix the oil and vinegar together and season well. Pour over the bees and serve.

SMOKED SALMON AND SCRAMBLED EGGS

The most delicious breakfast there is. Serve it with chilled Champagne or Buck's fizz. The secret of perfect scrambled eggs is to remove them from the heat just before they begin to set, as they will continue cooking on the plate. Have thin triangles of wholemeal (wholewheat) toast buttered and kept hot on warmed plates so that all that remains to be done once the eggs are cooked is to pop the cork.

Serves 2
6 medium-sized eggs
freshly ground black pepper
2 tbsp/25 g/1 oz butter
100 g/4 oz smoked salmon, cut into 1-cm (¼-in) squares
pinch of cayenne

1 Beat the eggs together with some pepper.

2 Melt the butter in a large heavy-bottomed pan over a low heat. Stir in the eggs and smoked salmon. Keep stirring, moving the spoon all over the bottom of the pan to prevent the eggs from sticking.

3 When the eggs are thick and creamy, pile them onto the hot toast, add a little cayenne and serve.

FROM THE DAIRY

LEEK AND STILTON BAKE

500 g/1 lb small leeks
6 eggs
1 slice wholemeal (wholewheat) bread, crumbed
2 tbsp cider vinegar
100 g/4 oz Stilton cheese

1 Preheat the oven to 200°C/400°F/Gas 6.

2 Trim and wash the leeks. Steam for 10-15 minutes. Lay them in a greased ovenproof dish.

3 Beat the eggs with the vinegar and breadcrumbs and crumble in the Stilton. Pour over the leeks and bake for 30 minutes until risen and golden.

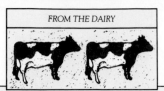

EGGS WITH CURLY KALE

Serves 2 or 4
500 g/1 lb curly kale
4 eggs
2 tbsp/25 g/1 oz butter
¼ cup/25 g/1 oz plain untreated (all-purpose) flour
300 ml/10 fl oz milk
½ cup/50 g/2 oz Cheddar cheese, grated
salt and freshly ground black pepper

1 Wash the kale and discard the stalks. Pack into a saucepan with a very little water, cover and cook slowly for about 20 minutes until tender. Drain and cut up roughly with a knife and fork. Put the kale in the bottom of a heatproof serving dish and keep warm.

2 Soft-boil the eggs.

3 Meanwhile, make the cheese sauce. Melt the butter in a pan and stir in the flour. Cook, stirring for a few minutes. Gradually add the milk. Continue to stir until the sauce has thickened. Add the cheese. When it melts, season.

4 Plunge the eggs in cold water and remove the shells. Lay them on the bed of kale and cover with the sauce. Heat the dish through in the oven or under the grill (broiler).

CHICORY (ENDIVE) SOUFFLE

3 heads of chicory (endive)
salt
juice of 1 lemon
3 tbsp/40 g/1½ oz butter
⅜ cup/40 g/1½ oz flour
300 ml/10 fl oz milk
½ cup/50 g/2 oz grated cheese
4 eggs, separated
1 tbsp dry brown breadcrumbs

1 Heat the oven to 200°C/400°F/Gas 6.

2 Trim the chicory and cook in salted water to which you have added the lemon juice. This will stop it discolouring.

3 When the chicory is tender, drain and set aside. When it is cool, press the water out from between the leaves with your fingers. Chop the chicory very finely.

4 Meanwhile, melt the butter in a heavy-bottomed pan. Stir in the flour. Remove from the heat and stir in the milk. Return from the heat and stir until the sauce has thickened. Add the cheese and cook for a further minute. Allow to cool.

5 When the sauce has cooled, mix in the chicory, then the egg yolks.

6 Whisk the whites until they form soft peaks and fold into the chicory mixture. Spoon into a greased soufflé dish and sprinkle the top with breadcrumbs.

7 Bake in the oven for 20-25 minutes until lightly set, well risen and golden on top. Serve this soufflé with a strongly flavoured salad, such as watercress garnished with slivers of orange.

GREEN PEA TARTS WITH POACHED EGGS

Makes 8 tarts

250 g/8 oz shortcrust pastry (enough for a single-crust pie)

1 kg/2 lb dried marrowfat peas, presoaked and cooked

4 tbsp/50 g/2 oz butter

salt and freshly ground black pepper

8 eggs

The tomato sauce

1-2 tbsp olive oil

1 onion, chopped

2 cloves garlic, chopped

400-g/15-oz can tomatoes

1 tbsp tomato purée (paste)

2 tsp dried oregano

salt and freshly ground black pepper

1 Preheat the oven to 200°C/400°F/Gas 6.

2 Roll out the pastry and line eight greased fluted tartlet pans. Prick with a fork and bake blind for 20 minutes until golden. Remove tart crusts from the oven and turn the heat down to 180°C/350°F/Gas 4.

3 In the meantime, make the tomato sauce. Heat the oil in a pan and add the onion and garlic. Cook until soft. Add the tomatoes, tomato purée, oregano and seasoning. Simmer for 5 minutes, then blend in a blender and keep hot.

4 Cook the peas until mushy, then drain and purée them in a blender. Heat the butter in a pan and stir in the pea purée. Season well with salt and plenty of black pepper. Divide the pea purée among the tart cases.

5 Poach the eggs until just set. Lift them carefully into the tart crusts and return to the oven for 2-3 minutes. Don't let the eggs harden. Serve each tart with a spoonful of tomato sauce.

AVOCADO SOUFFLE OMELETTE

Serves 2
1 green pepper
3 tbsp/40 g/1 ½ oz butter
1 ripe avocado
a dash of lemon juice
4 eggs, separated
salt and freshly ground black pepper

1 Deseed and slice the green pepper. Heat a little of the butter in a pan and fry gently until soft. Set aside.

2 Cut the avocado in half. Remove the stone and remove the flesh from the shell in one careful movement with a palette knife (spatula). Slice the avocado and sprinkle with lemon juice.

3 Beat the egg yolks and season with salt and pepper. Whisk the whites and fold the two together.

4 Heat half the remaining butter in a pan and pour in half the omelette mixture. Arrange half the avocado and green pepper on one side of it. When lightly set, fold the omelette in two, slide out of the pan and keep hot until you have made the second omelette in the same way.

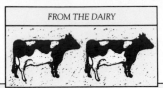
MUSHROOM OMELETTE SURPRISE

Serves 2 for a light lunch
100 g/4 oz mushrooms
about 150 ml/5 fl oz milk
1 tbsp butter
1 tbsp flour
1 tbsp grated Parmesan cheese
salt and freshly ground black pepper
4 eggs, separated

1 Peel or wipe the mushrooms and slice. Put them in a small, heavy-bottomed pan with a little of the milk and poach gently until very black and juicy. Remove the mushrooms with a slotted spoon and arrange them in the bottom of a shallow greased heatproof dish about 18 cm (7 in) in diameter.

2 Make a cheese sauce. Heat the butter in a pan and when it has melted, add the flour. Stir well and remove from the heat. Add the milk that the mushrooms have been cooked in and stir in enough extra milk (you may need a little more than 150 ml/5 fl oz) to make a thick sauce. Stir in the cheese and season well.

3 Beat the yolks into the cheese sauce. Whisk the whites until they form soft peaks and fold into the sauce.

4 Pour the mixture over the mushrooms and cook under a preheated grill (broiler) until the omelette is nearly set and golden on top.

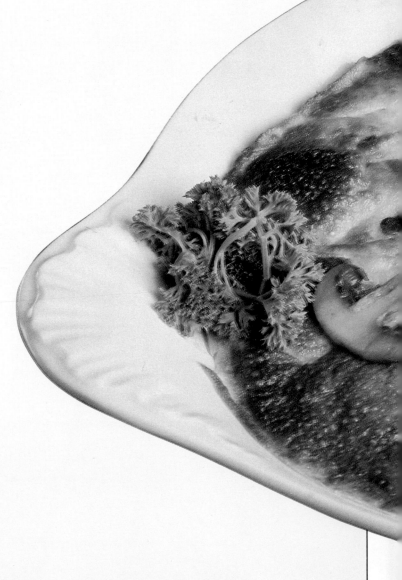

RICOTTA AL CAFE

This delicious bittersweet dessert is an Italian favourite. Eat it by dipping a spoonful of the cheese first into the coffee, then into the sugar.

1 cup/250 g/8 oz ricotta cheese
2 tbsp fruit sugar (fructose)
4 tbsp finely ground fresh coffee
2 tbsp brandy

1 Choose really moist ricotta cheese, or use fresh curd (cottage) cheese as a substitute. Press the cheese with half the sugar through a sieve to make it light and fluffy. Form into mounds on four individual dessert plates.

2 Sprinkle half the coffee over the cheese mounds. Spoon the remaining coffee and sugar onto the plates in two separate heaps at the side of the cheese and pour the brandy over the sweetened cheese.

PASKA

A heavenly dessert made in a flowerpot and traditionally served at Easter in Russia.

500 g/1 lb cream cheese
⅓ cup/50 g/2 oz sultanas (seedless white raisins)
6 tbsp/75 g/3 oz butter, softened
3 tbsp honey
3 egg yolks
230 ml/8 fl oz double (heavy) cream
½ cup/50 g/2 oz flaked almonds

1 Press the cream cheese through a sieve.

2 Soak sultanas in boiling water for 30 minutes. When they have plumped up, drain them and pat dry on kitchen paper.

3 Cream the butter, honey and egg yolks together in a mixing bowl. Gradually beat in the remaining ingredients until thoroughly blended.

4 Line one large or several small sterilized flowerpots with muslin (cheesecloth) and press the mixture into it (or them). Cover and weight the top (tops). Stand the flowerpot(s) in a bowl in a cool place to drain for 24 hours.

5 Turn out onto a plate, or individual serving dishes, and eat with fresh fruit and Amaretti (see p 69).

CREME CARAMEL

The caramel
4 tbsp fruit sugar (fructose)
4 tbsp water
The custard
600 ml/20 fl oz milk
a few drops of vanilla essence (extract)
4 eggs
40 g/3 tbsp fruit sugar (fructose)

1 Preheat the oven to 180°C/350°F/Gas 4.

2 For the caramel, put the sugar and the water in a heavy saucepan and stir over a low heat until the sugar has dissolved. Bring to the boil and boil until the syrup is golden. Pour the caramel into six individual moulds (or one large one) and swirl it around so that it coats the bottom and sides.

3 Bring the milk and vanilla essence to the boil in a saucepan. Remove from the heat.

4 Beat the eggs and sugar together in a bowl. Gradually add the hot milk, stirring all the while.

5 Strain or ladle the custard into the moulds. Stand them in a roasting tin half filled with hot water and bake for 45 minutes until set. Allow to cool and then chill. Don't turn out the crème caramel until you are ready to serve or it will lose its gloss.

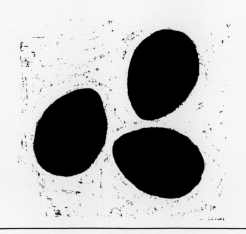

INDEX

INDEX